MW00413458

THIS ONE TREE

New Issues Poetry & Prose

Editor   Herbert Scott

Copy Editor   Curtis VanDonkelaar

Managing Editor   Marianne Swierenga

Assistant to the Editor   Kim Kolbe

Fiscal Officer   Marilyn Rowe

New Issues Poetry & Prose
The College of Arts and Sciences
Western Michigan University
Kalamazoo, MI 49008

First Edition, 2006.

ISBN-10   1-930974-61-2 (paperbound)
ISBN-13   978-1-930974-61-6 (paperbound)

Library of Congress Cataloging-in-Publication Data:
Peterson, Katie
This One Tree/Katie Peterson
Library of Congress Control Number: 2005936550

Art Director   Tricia Hennessy
Designer   Jason Punches
Production Manager   Paul Sizer
                       The Design Center
                       School of Art
                       College of Fine Arts
                       Western Michigan University

THIS ONE TREE

KATIE PETERSON

New Issues

 WESTERN MICHIGAN UNIVERSITY

For Molly and for Mike

Contents

Foreword

Readers of poetry live in times when critical expectations of poetry have never been higher or less reasonable, so permit this foreword to make an assumption consciously over the top: with every first book poetry ought to start all over again. Further, a first book should be written, and must read, as if a book had never been written before, as if the world is now what it always was: at its beginning and still largely untouched by apprehension, not yet something understood, not yet even attended to: in waiting. In this spirit a "first book" would somehow herald our very earliest influences. Crucial if entrenched ideas about apprenticeship and mastery may suppress this elemental truth.

Readers will find Katie Peterson's *This One Tree* to be just such a book. By looking at the world on behalf of the world, it offers its poetry up as a self-portrait of the world. And with what new powers of description, powers that balance all the warring senses of this currently discredited activity of poetry by committing to the genius of place, of the scribe, and of "scribble," or language itself. And with what visual command sponsored by what insistent powers of hearing, the senses at their beginning again as they, too, always were and always will be.

This writer of poetry has no interest in camps. She does not even give in to the current fashion of contending with fashion. Her poetry struggles to say what it is like to have our eyes opened by the world to which poetry devotes itself. It proceeds from its initial injunction—

> Be on the lookout
> for a wild symmetry
> Be on the lookout
> for weather lifting
> a man at the pharmacy
> shuddering asks
> do you have anything
> for my fast heartbeat?

—to a species and example of unstilled life, past imperative and on its own again and again:

> No one can pay attention for you.
> No one can ask the questions you ask
> how to ask

There are two current myths about seeing in poetry. The first is that seeing restores the world and the seer to themselves. That, as Simone Weil wrote, "absolute attention is prayer," absolving us of our indifference until—this from Eliot—"roses / had the look of flowers that are looked at." The second perhaps more prevalent myth is that seeing is the lackey of reason, of the five senses the most predatory, Wordsworth's "tyranny of the eye." Peterson has read deeply enough in poetry to take stock of these two myths and yet make her own determinations. For her attention is not only existential but also incremental, tuned to the daily, seasonal, yearly: to abiding creation. Attention may arrest the seer and the seen, but it also discovers continuation through release. Her poems understand both the rigors and the exultations of compounded study, a well as the primary longings—emotional, biological, spiritual—behind gaze.

Longing, or in Peterson's vocabulary, "desire," an open-ended plight, is what makes these poems so moving. A poetry willing to undergo individual desire requires a keen and reaching ear. This poet's prosodies and phrasings subdue internal and external noise without silencing tension. Her lyrics are aware enough of their own formal constraints that even when they close, they close open. The book ends with this memorable line:

> A look of life unable to sit still.

Not a look *at* life, but a look *of* life.

A few first books are original enough to make a difference. Katie Peterson's certainly has to this reader, who has not yet finished learning from it. In *This One Tree* from beginning to end is a poetry not indentured to idealism or skepticism but devoted to some marriage of faith and reality that makes both believable.

—William Olsen

Acknowledgments

Grateful acknowledgements are made to the editors of the following magazines, in which some of these poems appear:

Colorado Review: "Air"

Denver Quarterly: "Preludes and Fugues"

New Orleans Review: "The Tree" and "Grave"

Seneca Review: "Adam Waking"

What you look hard at seems to look hard at you.

—Gerard Manley Hopkins

I.

Air

Be on the lookout
for a wild symmetry
Be on the lookout
for weather lifting
A man at the pharmacy
shuddering asks,
do you have anything
for my fast heartbeat?
Be on the lookout
No clouds above
No air misty air
What must be unseen—
scent of ocean,
liquid-deep
Who would deny it?
Something was whelmed
Who might declare it?
Most life stayed put

Office

Orange, out the window,
maple sheds wrongly,
top first but off-kilter,
no right half, gone.
The left half leaving.
No one knows love
in the heart of another—
how much it is.
Totally orange.
Nothing of shading,
no red at edges—
somehow committed.
In a moment, committed.
Love, become waste,
ground, become darkness
deep within ground,
blister into magma.
Love becomes waste.
Refuse of dark skies,
mud made multicolored,
this lawn still mown,
halfleaves in the mower.

Song

This scattered removal:
leaves dried dry,
brief corners turned,
still interruptions.
Liftings. Upwardsnesses.
Those earlyfallen,
where have they gone?
None on the groundswell
of freshdirted root.
None on the lawn, lying.
Trunk still so dark.
Branches spindles.
Care at the base.
Care not fresh love.
Clock in the distance,
face in these branches,
how sounds grow long,
lessen the hours
that go on—
The quarters of hours.
Taken away.

Little Elegy

Out one's own window
nothing turns partial,
yellow stays yellow,
day keeps blue.
As for the leaves,
what's strong continues,
little hangs lightly,
instead holds on.
Chill gets here late.
It won't stay.
Ask it again.
Ask the clear absence.
Silly green grief,
piece of self,
the world already turned
cold for you.
It ran you down.
It had you whole.

Memory

in thickest glasses
one left alone
blown clear across crisply
sniff of old paint and new
one left alone
Who moved the bench?
one left alone
so much sunlight as
(one left alone)
if layers of dust
(one left) edged (alone)
sunlit like junk
noticed these things
with senses left over
call it redness
prior to rust
noticed these things

For You

At two-thirty, and three,
in dark you wake
the other person.
You might say for beauty:
moon's crooked light,
half-opened.
Whatever convinces.
Colder and likelier,
what they don't know—
each heart the set of:
waiting, one tree,
one evening,
one country road.
These leaves ungrown
purposefully.
How could you know?
Seasons reversed.
What should you tell them?
Spring unprepared for.
Go where I'm not.

For Elsewhere

Someone ought to
know where we are.
Then there were no
signs or family
homes save yours,
isolate and familiar.
World green.
Woods thick.
The lake so clean
we drank it.
We were together.
We were similar.
I remember how
you drove the car.
The mirror so ajar,
it rusted wrong,
and no one told you.
Someone should have.
Hypochondriac world,
where we need a person
to hold our hands
up to the light,
and say, they are the same.
They match.
They are right.

For S

The man
who loves
the sound of his
voice singing.
Evergreens made crisper
by the wet cold,
crisper elsewhere.
The ones here roughs
of those forms,
those my elsewheres.
Better to gather
(as you say) piney
cones the shape of
singing.
Better steal something
someone else sang,
store it up quietlike,
for blank white winter.

Tree

Weeks too early
one colors completely
unaccompanied in the garden.
Something not right.
One alone, so lifting, so
itself, so lifted, yellow leaves look
lighter, act lighter, are!
A laugh released
hits walls, hears hollows—
walls of brick, late leaf shade,
permanent, darker when wet.
A ping pong ball
let loose in church,
church empty, preaches
emptiness—
                sweet ricochet
makes whatever world
there is sound sided.

Job

Sound of a rake,
many-pronged, dozened
across the crisp dark.
Go towards it now.
Ask the old man
(true he might laugh)
what you can do,
here, what accomplish?
He might refuse you.
This world comes alone,
take it that way.
Piles to make.
That's not your job.
Light them on fire.
Light the whole hillside.
What of the rake?
So soundly steeped,
ear in this darkness
wherever it moves,
to empty trees:
rake in the branches.

II.

At the Very Beginning

When I named you I was on the verge
of a discovery, I was accumulating

data, my condition was that of a person
sitting late at night in a yellowing kitchen

over steeping tea mumbling
as his wife remotely does the laundry.

My condition was that of a mathematician
who cannot put the names to colors,

who, confusing speaking and addition,
identifies with confidence the rain

soaked broad trunked redwood tree (whose
scent releases all of winter) saying as he passes *one*

Adam and Eve in the Morning

In a time of great anxiety,
the two of them wondered was it time.

It was spring's seam with winter.
Snow turned to water in the gutters

with a river sound imported from a wilder location.
A pair, some songbirds, made their nest in the dryer

crying all morning was it time. On the recording
of the song the woman played, birds cried as well.

There had been applications, there were tests.
Their histories were the same all over,

all of them demanded was it time.
Something happened as they didn't look,

at the end of night, having a domestic argument.
They had been having it for days,

the noise and the decisions and the light,
still they believed

the open-all-night-club must close some time.
When it did, last evening got let out

into the street and all they thought
was, it was time long ago, it was already time.

The birds in the dryer are still asleep,
we do not know exactly where they are,

in fact they may be safely in the eaves
by now. What are they singing?

It sings ourselves, before we have a chance.
The day broke long before its time.

Adam and Eve at Noon

For years you wonder whether the architecture
will hold. And then it doesn't, and then you know.

Or how when I put my hand through your hair
I am putting my hand through the memory

of your red hair, in the movies,
at that one time, in that one place.

There was no tree where we came from.
There were only the hillside grasses (these

never needed names), the faint
cry of a towhee, the comforts of science fiction.

Someone read us through our childhood.
How long have these things been untouched?

Though the noon shines flat upon you
and makes you want to move,

stay in the first place you ever were,
it is the best place.

Backtrack

Backtrack of weather against the grain of season,
backtrack of green maple against its redder brothers.

The best thing about now is that it will not be always.
You will assimilate yourself into my narrative,

red apple solitary on the desk.
Someone told me not to be a student.

Don't put so much emphasis on the fall.
Red apples so blithely in season.

That the body could be coaxed into the soul,
and seat itself, and find something to eat—

Backtrack of *experience* against the grain of *philosophy*,
loving the world and leaving it alone—

Eve (Vows)

Put this wish on the wing of one short breath:
to be lost and free, lost and free.

The shepherds have no last name and wander freely
between what we call countries in the night.

It is a far cry from here. Here
young women carrying water to the wedding

walk silent on saris rolled and unrolled
ahead and behind by an older generation,

fabric dyed so dark bright color comes off
on those hands which hold it fast against the road

to the river and back again, hands full of bowls
full of water, which must not drip upon the silk,

the cobalt blue and sky of the silk.
The sacred cow enjoys her lily garland

dumbly. Everyone wishes on her all day.

Regret

Going backwards with great effort
like a gear shifting on a childhood

bike, a painter paints out
a bowl of fruit

that refuses to balance the picture.
When I saw you last you lacked

decorum but I am not sure
how you showed it.

Let me speak a moment
before this labor disappears.

Let me tell about the fruit shifting
under its own weight.

It seemed less true
as I tried to capture it

because it had changed
from what I first saw.

The invisible hurts most,
the forgotten makes no sense

because it is invisible.
No rip in the fabric but

there should be. Not this
canvas empty save everything else.

Adam and Eve in the Evening

Our animal is so peaceful, he looks as if he were dead.
Tell me again how we met.

Tell me the story of your life.
I've caught something. Are you coming down with it?

The workmen outside work for no set time.
Close your eyes. What color are my eyes?

Tell me whether I should wake you early.
Asleep the animal looks less like a cat.

Tell me what to think.
Whether the weather will be fine tomorrow.

What color the thunder might render
the sky. Even if it won't be.

In summer your ribs show through your shirt
almost. Say

there has never been another,
that it is time for me to take your glasses

off, that I should never wake you.
How long have you been living in my breath?

Look at me like you want me to speak.
I do not know that there are things you think.

Twilight Adam

A light breeze,
the sound of coinage.

How did things
get this way,

arranged, particular?
Who placed the lavender

in this one window,
scented across

what was once perfect,
trio of trees?

I don't believe
in gut feelings,

don't believe that
we are likenesses.

My hands grow raw,
writing this—

Adam and Eve in Bed

Where have you hidden the toolkit, the umbrellas?
The least we could do is keep our things in order.

The least we could do is keep each other in order.
You mislaid me last night and now I hurt.

I prefer games of randomness to games of chance.
You prefer night to morning but cannot choose.

You like the idea of preference but cannot choose.
You lie awake choosing not choosing all night.

More animals gather then, they love this house at night.
We used to discuss them until we fell asleep.

Who could fly the longest distance,
and who could swim.

If we had information about fins or wings
If we knew how a body carried itself alone

Have you been out playing games of chance?

Adam Waking

We chose this animal to be our pet.
His indifference allowed us to sleep.

Cat, who made your ears bend back,
who made you lazy as quick?

Who made you work?
It is a wonder any sun is left.

Still it is always so abrupt.
Sleep like an umbrella going up,

clumsy like a broken umbrella coming down,
this waking, and into what?

I did not ask to be afraid.
I did not ask for pleasure, but there it was,

it exfoliated at its own leisure,
grew until it was all that was—

The brief interruption of who I am
interrupts and punctuates the day

I always assumed that I would share—
Cat who cut the sun down from the sky

and then responsible put it up again?
There must be one of us that you prefer.

Locus Poenitentiae

Dusk: trees wear their frames so lightly they
almost disappear. Elephant

slips from elephant and becomes not.
Birds slip from themselves and fly away.

The sky eats us in shades of blue
shading us eaten in crepuscular hues.

We say the names of things to make them
still, say them again to make them move.

They still again. Dark goes into dark.
Birds wing up. Their flying falls from them, their

shadows off. Red birds the color of rust.
Deer pace, retreat, and become lost,

poached by wood-dark, not ours, never possessed.
You wear your name so lightly you

almost disappear, lifting up your hands.
What we call *the lifting up of hands.*

When it was time for us to undo all
the things that we had ever named

we lost our nerve. The evergreen dark
coniferous. The sky might hit our heads,

new trees might seed and grow, our selves might soft
quiet and resolved. Remembered to this spot—

and as I raved and grew more fierce and wild
and as I cried and knowledge slipped from me—

I became all voice with a peculiar ring,
mere accompaniment my clear-voiced companion,

Dusk I was, worn so lightly: (no one missed me): sing:

Lexicon

Down the ridge, towards the green estuary
the watery fields take that green inland

having their way with it, until where we were once
ends short, abrupt, at angles with that land

where one slight path crumbles the fieldgrassed hill
diagonal, where one slight path stands still—

*

Measured from beginning to end all grasses there
stay green and equal, some seasonless intent

at odds with calendar, at odds with light
that sees no two waverings equally—

*

No words adhere to all you were and are.
Calendric, temporal, this first world returns

perfect, fastidious when it comes at all
to mind these autumn elsewhere days

when full and rich the green and yellow
curtains newly hung breathe like twin lungs.

Outside the great craniums of sycamores
fill with wind, hollow themselves, and rise—

Creation from Chaos

In the great river gorges
a misguided bird

breaks the egg of the world
unceremoniously,

unclear whether eating
or hatching is in order.

The trees so full of gibbons
no flying thing can nest.

And the gibbons will not rest.
Screechings accumulate

like round peelings
of bark, seasonal and shed.

Everyone desperately present.
The accident begins.

Prophecy

Shadows deepen
the Latin inscription above a gated archway

on the ground shadows sharpen
because the leaves have sharpened

their pointedness grown excruciating
thinned to brittle

skeletal and upturned
like our palms will be in winter

asking each other—*when*
the ice air grown incomprehensibly

thinner, then, we will know
how things were better

we were better suited
to each other

though not closer
not as close—

The tree was red.

Story

The animals marched. Nothing could disturb them,
deer and elephants equal in double file

across the worked silk brocade we purchased together
from the marketplace in the city center.

The colors of it edged towards blue fresh water
and edged away from the maize of the horizon

which was, that day, the same gold as the leaves
surrendered early by the newly planted young elm tree

in a perfect circle around its raised root base.
Those matched the color of a swinging traffic light

listing above in some sudden gust of wind
whose home was somewhere, close, marine, and north,

in which the neighborhood wrens took flight
and quickened in a new and double task—

to fly, and to keep warm and not keep still,
distributing themselves through all the streets

that led us here, where this could be bought.
This man did not know the maker of its light

blue threads and purple threads and gold
crossed by other hands into each other.

He offered us instead some reckless story
about how it fell into his hands that we

could not believe. We wrapped our cloth and left.

III.

The Tree

When I was young and alone the afternoon became
a plum tree in the darkest
corner of the orchard
fruit dense, equally distributed
on the lowest boughs and the highest branches.
Scent of it like a whistle, like a branching hand
of whistles going off.
Scent not yet turned to rot.

Those branches black and thick
as if fruit did not interrupt
but continued them, handfuls of purples
bruised with red like the heat of a hand,
some low enough to hang
past the smooth waist of the tree as if the lower trunk
had been uprooted and dipped, whitewashed, as it was,
to the visible roots—

Whitewash meant the tree was sick.
Something must be done to preserve
this afternoon. There is something I must do.
I am eating all the fruit I can.
Still it is not enough. Wide-eyed before
what could not be kept.
It is today that you may eat your fill.
And so I do. I do not know what else to do.

I did not know my heart until it was wrenched.
Whitewashed, the scored surface of the condemned tree
stood muffled, as if there could be
a sound it wanted to make.
Still I believe there was something to be done
I did not do, where I myself stood,
tallying the fruit I ate
undecided, unmoved, to this day—

The Tree

Church bells at the same time as sirens.
Cold feet in the wake
of someone else's umbrella.
Wet leaves like footprints
of some imaginary animal
too unfriendly to be imagined.

Cold morning, years past,
I leaned upon the great pine tree
we called the great pine tree
and in its branches always
the remnants of a house.
Why take down what might be

useable, one parent said. The other
said nothing. Still we never climbed,
or never built. Over years
the triangular frame grew wet and even
the wood became contagious rust.
When we played we played around it.

Cold winter and a broken pattern
of warm days on the blank canvas
of inevitable horizon.
Once I sent myself into winter alone.
Now it is dexterity that helps me
imagine the tree, not courage. Never that.

The Tree

There are plenty of girls
who like you,
and I am one of them,
but I have
a lover, and he is careful,
and I am afraid you won't be.

Orange tree filling the small
yard with all its scent
and waxy dark forest green leaves.
How do you know what
I like? Orange tree,
no one had to guess your origin. At night

you were a shadow
of yourself but more substantial
that way. Orange
in midsummer, oranges
in winter, orange peel
in every single cup of tea.

My mother said
it was always better that way.
Talked and talked of what
I wouldn't like. But I
didn't know, orange tree,
never knew. Don't know now.

The Tree

To be betrayed. To be laid
bare in the shade of eucalyptus
arching over some mottled rock.
To be laid out so no action was
appropriate, possible, or true.
No task done in the shade

of eucalyptus, in the grove near
the house in which I grew.
This was never hypothetical.
The secret I hid was something
I didn't do, would not do.
My secret wrecked me. You

wandered off, untrue,
leaf of eucalyptus unfallen
bark of eucalyptus unshed.
This one tree intact. While others
mimicked the autumn that occurred
elsewhere, on a harsher coast.

You became more lost, and lost me so,
I had no choice but to lose
you and never lose (not once) bark
of eucalyptus, never the scent of it,
never that medicinal dirt, still
like no healing power, none at all.

The Tree

The Japanese maple bought on a
whim at a fair grew right there
on the dark edge of the front yard,
spread its branches and was
never strong. Turned colors
no one asked it for.

Each year that green grew dark,
darker than it was, how dark
no one could say as we could not
see all those years together.
Still it was easy to know. A narrative
that darkens makes itself known.

Stars like flowers the shape of
stars were those leaves of that
Japanese maple. In my dream
a man helped me climb
a mountain called *Praise* in Latin
unhampered by paths hampered by trees.

I loved his singing
and his gentleness.
Each investigation became a part
of the path. He said
my whole name as if
to take it into his mouth.

What was not there was this: nothing
the shape of a Japanese maple,
branches a marriage of willow
and spiny fir. What was not
there: marriage of trails at some
top-heavy head. Only one way up.

53

The Tree

Japanese maple, so well tended,
how do you keep your smallest branches
orderly? Can you keep them strong?
Or are they weak, abundantly,
doing whatever the trunk tells them
to? Nights looking at you

in the thick lamplight you were you
and your own shadow of light.
Nights stopping here, there was
no need to choose, you were
what home was, you were
my lexicon of belonging, my

own location. Though I regretted
all I never once regretted you.
Nights in the garden I realized I
never arrived, always returned.
Often I touched you inadvertently
on my known way in unseen.

Nothing meant anything here.
What I want is to have chosen
already what to do.
In this mirror the wreck of moon
becomes its wrong half equally
distributed upon the whole room.

Aubade of the Tree

To hold off the morning you slept
To hold off the morning I stared at you
I read a book and then another book
And one was *philosophy* and one was *poetry*
And neither put me to sleep and neither spoke
To hold it off then I went to the window
Where the trees arranged themselves
In the electric backlit last act blue like tangled wires
Nothing kept me there and so I slept

In this house I wake up with the trees
I stand and I stand level with their trunks
In the childless yard next door they stand up straight
In the populated yard they have grown crooked
And two have hooked themselves around each other
In occult friendship and at night
They make an arch some story must explain

But neither night nor morning occurs
The sycamores drip with referential power
The way their branches disintegrate in air
Some guarantee they will be refreshed
The sky they point to is and it is new
No window frames these branches alone
But takes in everything, takes this one tree in
(Which is a sycamore, here before I came)
As if in responsibility, as if in thoughtfulness
Which no house truly holds
Except the house where someone stays awake

55

Grave

One could do worse than an unmarked stone.
In leaf time it looks even more gray
and in the snow
who knows how covered it could remain.

No one to visit and no one to know.
The noon sits down on every stone
the same. Hard noon,
hot stone. You have to touch it to know.

It could be in any yard at all.
One could do worse
than have it here,
and leave it unvisited most of all.

The rain has no object, it falls and falls.
One could do worse some lost spring
to be in love,
love someone most near the smoothest stone,

look at one person and softly think,
wherever you are I will know
I put you there
I will think on my stone

when I am gone and there's nothing to know—

IV.

Aubade (Winter)

When I talk to you I remember winter.
I remember winter. I will not talk to you again.

As if the mind could find a greener melancholy,
one tree made the darkness stand up straight.

On the same breath the words of you and winter.
In your words how one winter once was.

The pine tree fell and the house stood still.
Intermittent power kept us all on edge
even when lit and all the homework done,
the threat of it. What was said was meant.
Storms came for months after they left.
My father swearing and the lights gone out.

Never. The vegetable patch
turned into a pool and neighbors came.
They razed the fields and the town
grew up. We grew indifferent to our lack
of what we first had and everything at once.
Notice changes and the heart goes out.

The man who sold glass animals isn't dead.
I kept him in business until I moved
away, remembered as long as I had room
inside myself glass horses I kept broken.
The roses named for women lined his walk.
His gate shrieked shut in the winter rain.

Father's tended to by someone else.
The trees he planted with his own hand,
redwoods, add to the value of his land,

which he will sell without asking me.
Still your voice is the voice of someone driving
straight to California without stopping

I'm jealous of calm purpose of all kinds.
Nothing I think stays thought or put.

Weather changes and is gone.
You see I am a mystery to myself.

I forget how I never wanted to speak.
I hate the world that happened just to me.

Aubade (Quartet)

If you came at night like a broken king
you would be elsewhere and
in England, you would be younger,
you would have more diligence.
Everything read a thing reread.

And so I thought—not to mistake the world—
And so I thought—snow falling quick
light now always on the unread book—
not to mistake one person for another,
not to mistake one flower for another—

The boy slept all night in the ivy.
All night the girl read in the open window.
She read away. *Desire*. It is
an open-ended word. One silent letter.
Someone always leaving it alone.

And the last word in the book was Time.
No, the last word in the book
was One—the last word
she remembered was Time,
and she remembered and remembered it.

Aubade (Casaubon)

Beautiful questioner, the trees are tormenting me again.
I have traded in the affection I knew
for someone responsible, if somewhat oblivious,

who understands me and keeps that understanding.
But I still walk home at two in the morning,
the street slightly luminous too long.

A held breath of moderate amount.
We have long since ceased paying for our own drinks,
if you know what I mean, questioner,

now we take turns. At least you are the kind
who doesn't pick up the phone when we're in bed.
But we were fully clothed, speaking of *Middlemarch*.

Questioner, you had a hat on your head.
Allergies. The trees shed their flowers and you got well.
The name shouted in the street

stopped. And so, you went to sleep.
The hedge overgrew the fence, the rosemary,
but its scent did not provoke me.

Some other scent must have, provoked me, question-asker,
your arms intentionally thin, outstretched,
whether preaching to me or listening, feminine.

Preludes & Fugues

The slow construction of a house.
Rain and a bicycle, a helmet like a hat.
A prelude to rain, a night without it.
Now wrong turns in the car not retractable.
This consistent retracing the block,
a butterscotch hard candy still in the mouth.
The tongue and something on the tongue.
You have been called back   You have
no choice   Your name is known here
say the same old bells, the rusted clappers
The house you thought would never be finished,
the fields that should be long destroyed,
have been saved for nothing in your absence,
for a long corridor of pictures unrecognized.
The piano played brilliantly with one hand.
Here is the service for you to attend.
You will find that you know the music.
In your dream I was a train conductor.
In your dream I said You Know Nearly Nothing.
The place was Ventimiglia in late spring, a country's border
Here the border is between Eve and Day,
the border lies between Day and Day After.
You will find the service has begun.
As for the silence it has yet to be.
Everything is prelude to it. And yes,
and after it, is folded in.
The bell goes back and forth. The sound is red.
You will find that you know the music.
The wind blows back and forth across your name.

You Asked

I began to tell you something and began
by telling you something else, about
the actual bearbaiting that we saw
twin bears chained up and some
dogs let loose
looked up at them in the dead wet moat of the old castle in the town
called Ceské Krumlov that we went to visit
because it had been called the second
most historic town by UNESCO (after Venice).
I know that I forgot to talk about
the cold cake and the sodas that we had
in the tiny candy-striped café floor tiled with circus animals.
We were in Ceské Krumlov. But first
we were staying in Ceské Budejovice
because one cannot stay in the oldest restored town.
It has been made into a restored town
not for staying in but looking at.
We stayed an hour away in an old town
that wasn't as historic but was
still old—they made the stuff to build
to fix and not to last the way they did
ages ago. The tilers tiled roofs
and floors they way they'd done before,
forever as long as anyone could remember,
like that crooked path of tiles with animals
in that small cafe kitchen leading to the doorway
at which it all became rough brick.
But that was not in Ceské Budejovice at all.
The pensione where we stayed
cost six dollars for a bed and food,
soft porn curtains of an obscene pink
a shade we drew in the middle of the day.
The train was bumpy. There was no other way

to Ceské Budejovice, from which we took
a bus the next day to Ceské
Krumlov to see the sights
that had inspired us to come and see.
I know I told you about that bus
that left us there from nine until four
which was the reason we had to go to see
an exhibit of the paintings of Egon Schiele
that for no reason we could figure out
cost fifteen dollars in the Czech Republic
in 1995 when everything
was cheap.
Even the rich had to go out of town
to pay more than an American quarter
for a cup of coffee and a roll.
I know that we got lost in Ceské Krumlov
which was a hollow and subconscious town,
the houses empty and restored to be
empty as they once were when the town
was old and poor. I know we stumbled in-
to a vast control room which controlled
the lights and music in the heart of town
and seemed small from the street.
I remember a gate
that closed upon us in the castle's heart,
a gate that led to graves and monuments
whose restoration was still going on
and that we sat and ate the lunch we got
from Ceské Budejovice's heart,
its market, where we had gone when dawn
woke us through the lace bordello curtains
from good dreams to a bad breakfast that looked good
as it was foreign and included coffee.

I know that we got out of town,
of Ceské Krumlov and that on the bus
I met an architect who was American
wearing black leather with a black walkman
who spoke to me while he listened to music
and stressed the fact that he was an architect,
that in fact he had built a building
I must have known, near my hometown.
He was at least seventy.
Then we got back to town.
And walked the couple-dozen block walk home
from the station to our bordello pensione
with its bad sweet morning meal. On the way
we spoke loudly to each other
of how we were so sick of all the sweets
we'd eaten. But had we had
that much? We cried No More Treats
We Can't Have Them
We Can't Have Any More!
I have reached the shout in the dark
from an upstairs window. The torso of a stranger,
in a pensione much richer than ours,
leaned into the night air we had to breathe
and spoke to us in our own language,
spoke as we ran away: What can't you have?
And this is what I have been trying to say.

Mammoth Lakes

Everywhere we go
children are telling their parents what they know.
The climate of encyclopedic places.
The shape and weight of the human brain.
How far I can run. This is the place for this,
for small vacations, everyone along
without much planning with a lot of gear.
Tackle shops and places not to cook.
So seasonal the high school makes you sad.
Where we stay is made of dark fake wood,
called the Wood, or Woodlands, or the Trees
depending on address and size of place
size of place depending on address.
Familiar, unremarkable, not home.
On the river I think of all I know.
How to hold a thing and keep it held.
How to snap a fly box slyly shut
with one hand gone.
Left-handed there are things I badly learned.
Too many to speak of now. Hard not to think
of all there was I never got to right.
The wind is friend and sounds like it is young.
The water is just melted
in my mind. Touching it, its narrative of snow.
Last night you told me something that began
My Father Was Asleep
and then you smiled.
In fact it was long after he had slept.
Forgetting he was in fact mine too.
We had been talking music. You had said
All My Favorite Singers Couldn't Sing.
Then you asked me to sing.
I chose Don't Think Twice It's Allright,

saying, you can have it angry or sad
like Dylan did. You had it sad.
The fake wood deck suspended in the trees
above a spooky golf course that looked green
even in black dark.
The developed ridge.
The ridges where development didn't take
in clearer sight, unlit lines of dark.
You looked at me like I was someone else.
Distracted into anecdote you were
not distant. I don't know what you were.
But laughing made that thing retract itself.
I had been in
the story you had told.
And now the river is not far from him.
Our father. If it was, he couldn't go.
His voice involves a lot of breath.
He keeps the car in sight. His shoes are clean.
You are somewhere and I wish
you weren't. The mountain looms
and has no sound at all.
Right here is named for lakes we've never seen.
I don't know what about me wants you here
or wants to say
in exact words
I have spent this afternoon

and at least half of a windy evening
fishing with my father in overfished waters.
I must tell you the fish are gone or small.
Come here. I do not fear that you are lost.
If that singing is you, you're yards away.

Translation (from Petrarch 141)

In the hot times only
the butterfly seeking heat wants light
will fly into another's eyes. Then it dies.
Then that person hurts.

I go to light in eyes
where Fate is. There's what's sweet
Since when was Reason ever prized
by Love? Desire always hated it.

What I see is how I'm shunned.
There I am and know I'll die.
Against it I'm nothing strong. Pain is.
Love dazzles, and so does,

I explain another's pain and not my own.
My soul dies blind saying Yes—

*

In misplaced spring the fragile butterfly
for so long submerged will chose to fly
into a well that is a human eye.
There it drowns and dies.

I am that thing. I go to my
dark fate, will myself into that well
where no light is and Reason
never went. It never went, it feared Desire.

What I see, takes me whole.
When I am there, it is to die.
Did Love fake this darkness? Must I hurt
myself before I find another self?

The well knows nothing. As for my soul
even her heart is blind when she says Yes—

*

It was some other spring. The butterfly
curious with wings chose to fly
eyeward, in fact into these eyes.
Then it died. O there was sight and hurt.

Now it is my turn to light
into the eyes of fate, to call them sweet,
to praise how Reason never earned
the praise of love, was hated by Desire.

I was already seen and taken in.
How can I live when I know how to die?
However dazzles Love I must explain
everything but what I am myself,

which is what I have seen. It is my soul
that dies. It does so saying Yes—

*

I missed spring. I, the butterfly
everyone knew cocooned. I chose to fly
summerward into a pair of eyes.
I died. I am speaking to you dead.

I said I was. I said I went
darkly to fate, the sockets of the eyes
darkened. I saw where Reason was.
Where it never went I named Desire.

It would not have me halved. It took both parts.
It took me broken until I died
brokenly. Without the story of myself
the trajectory I thought belonged to me.

Each day a death I have assented to.
The spring I missed must come in heat again.

Aubade (Spring)

What broke from you?
I know what broke from me: forsythia.
Dogwood in decaying light.
A large black crow in the library trees.

A hand broke from you. I saw it break.
And recklessness, which breaks to be destroyed.
You used it up to use it up for good.
You meant to have no more of what it was.

But these were things I could not see.
I went into the house, you
fled into the yard. I left my shoes out.
I became a person without shoes.

And in the middle of the night,
a waltz broke from me—
a memory I saw move across a room.
I begrudge you that.

As it was you always asked me what I
was thinking. What broke from you?
What self went out to go back in again?
What answered question? What chastening?

V.

The World

It was bound to happen.
Affect on one coast, intellect
on another: under the plane
the world like the inside of a geode.
Split apart. In places sparkly.

You were nowhere you looked
for yourself. Your back ached
with looking. Affect
left behind, intellect
not yet found, and not yet landed,

you stretched back without relaxing.
One day there was a decision
to be made. The next,
nothing. The same dense light
low on the winter strip mall

where ski clothes always
are in season. The music store
where nothing sounds good,
not even what you wanted, going
in, what you knew you loved.

Death changed nothing.
The world became more this way,
I think I would say,
if I was given speech,
after the first household

cat was put to sleep, after
they told me and I cried.
We have not yet touched down.
What you think in the sky
stays in the sky.

Song

I was given more than I required.
Goat cheese, a cranberry skirt.
More still that I did not want.
Two days above the ocean, a flat rock
on which to eat. More still
than that, the unexpected scent of one gardenia.

The zipper on my favorite sweater
replaced. Saved wisdom teeth.
I was given summer again and again,
given fall in the place it must
have been made. Given clover, shadowy,
the yard that made me think the world was mine.

Given two trees, given from their start,
Japanese maples, one red and one green,
their leaves like insects satelliting branches,
and I was given branches,
which were sometimes cut, which grew
again, redirected themselves correctly up.

I was given the company of friends,
the picture of a crucifixion tree,
well-meant, I was given a new name,
but I never used it, sweet alyssum
flocking around the frozen orange tree
in some crazy season, never, though it stained

my previous years with who
I had not been, I was given
who I had not been,
and I received that absence
like a light, a visitation, which is what it was.
That I could make a thing happen to me.

The Afternoon

Each of us has one grief that means
we are not fit for life.
Hers was her hair.
She changed it once and never changed again.
Mine is how I say what I don't mean.

I say: she never sewed one thing for me.
Her fingers lost a ring when I was born.
Star sapphires alternated with fake diamonds.
The latest afternoon I ever knew
not yet turned to evening she

slept through. Rust turned pine needles,
torn green checkered quilt dragged farther out.
Her sleeping. Suspended curls of willow bark.
Sun fell behind those trees and came up stars.
I very well may have been happy then.

Something was borrowed. The trees were once
an orchard harvested and picked
seasonally: plums oranges pears.
Long before we came half them were cut.
Is half an orchard orchard enough?

A painting that I love now has no shape.
Its field of orange disintegrates into a field
of yellow. Paper, reproduced, and thin
it looks how it must have once been, stretched
upon a canvas. When I watch it in the light

adhering to the wall I chose for it,
a shuttering of sun
crosses the painting and makes no sense.
The colors marry like they wanted all along.
Half themselves, they're gone.

Song (In Winter)

The birds were never singing in the dryer.
I don't know why I thought they were.
In fact they were somewhere in the eaves,
they were singing through
the rotted pipes, the air ducts, the unfinished
uninsulated walls. They were never

where I thought they were,
lost inside the house
where they shouldn't have been. Their song never spun.
When they sang they sang through bitter
air outside. It found itself
here. A discovery to no one but me.

The day we watched a seablue bird
dip himself into the icecold water
of the frozen gutter next door, out the bedroom window
again and again, thin floating panes of ice
broke
each time he dipped his head and shook it off.

He was refrozen and he dipped again
his whole blue beating self
his beating heart
visible. It was inside himself.
So cold, he was farther from dead
than anything I've seen since then.

A few mornings ago I got up early,
Closed the bedroom door, and fell
asleep while reading
nothing punctuated by remembering.
I woke again:
The sound of water shaking off a razor.

Under your breath you were singing
a song incomprehensible to me.
What woke me was the razor,
not the singing, though I went back to sleep,
though easily I slept again thinking
try me try me I can even sleep through that.

The Conversation

Rain-soaked, the mottled bark
of the flowering pear darkened
past its texture's vanishing.
My confessions always provoke
someone else's confessions.
Why do you stand in the kitchen

if you don't want to talk?
The changing light of morning
goes back and forth
as if it had already been
one whole mixed-up day.
Pear leaves tracked in

and out. The conversation
continues between windows.
Pear leaves shed around the house.
I thought by earning the world
I might have myself.
I thought you were listening.

Growth for this one tree meant
staying still. Still means
what it did then. Hardened
into a random texture
from the inside out and as we speak.
As if I could speak my heart.

The Road

Tell me the truth and then leave me alone.
Driving through, driving
through a grove of eucalyptus.
Torn, the bark of eucalyptus.
The car whips air into itself.

All through the green winter
the beavers thrive, and wreck the right flood plain
damming it wrongly.
The road becomes impassable enough
to be a nuisance.

Tell me the truth.
On the way home, on the way there
when I leave here will I be the same?
What do I take
when I take pigment into my skin?

Did that turn of the road
that I had feared
finally find its way into my hand
which seems to keep things like letters and numbers,
seems to keep them when they disappear?

Song

It wintered in you. It did.
Wintering. There was no cure
for it, it wintered.
You are a cider press,
you kept it as long as you could.

But then it wintered,
and then it was dead.
Under the whitewashed apple
tree you wrote your name:
again: your name was winter:

even your name was
dead. That fall you wrote
it: again and again.
Driving through the fog,
on the windshield, you wrote

so it would stay there,
later, past the moment
you were lost and could not see,
past that, past unfindable.
But it wintered in you,

giving you winter,
as an illness, as the rust
on a left-out cider
press, or some other,
mechanical, it did, it did.

Song

It is best to be patient and calm.
It is best to look for one's heart,
to look
for one's heart and find a button,
finally, to fasten oneself up.

There is no danger, not now,
when the world gets ahead of itself
and dries out the magnolia.
Wood-chips in a light wind.
And the sun spread thin.

Take a walk, there is no danger.
Walk (when you are tired of the river)
across it, all the way to the public garden,
which you will hit
in twilight if you time it right,

and the world goes green,
except for the roses. There is no
danger, nothing inevitable.
The world goes green for everyone,
sometimes, it is best

to let it, best to take
a quick train home
wherever it is you live, best
to stop forever looking out of windows.
Cordelia said nothing

to her father, sending herself
out for him. Noticed how the corn
grew high. It is best to say nothing.
Look for the sculpture
until it becomes found.

Song

Overnight the steps took wet pollen into their grain
and yes it stuck.
The tree next door, some kind of maple,
still branched like a choice.
The doors to the cellar mossed over, still, unlatched.

Someday someone will recall yesterday
as a day when leisure held so much impatience.
Spring world, but windy: a scarf was not enough.
Then the light shut down.
All I was afraid to say receded.

No one should drag a rocking-chair into the yard
today.
No one should ever speak.
We should stay inside, we should treat our allergies.
Solving problems with sleepy drinks.

Chamomile: a flower with wood dissolved
in it. We lifted the bag of tea
back and forth between our cups until it broke.
This evening you watched my hand cross a dish in water.
You took it shook it dried it put it away.

Song

You must believe in spring.
The hedge falls from the hedgerow and changes
everything.
Where the cat was once the chair
is now without the cat.
How he did bend back when he could
into the curve of it to catch
rare sunlight in the winter months and dare
think of himself as a warm noble thing,
endowed in a peculiar dream I
can only write of now to say a human Yes.
Still you must believe that we are all
closer and closer to unpremeditated speech.

The Way Things End

The way things end, they have no reason in them.
They have no reason, then they disappear.
Waking from a nap into a night,
some admission the day was beyond repair.
Amid the circulation of warmer air.

My cousin lived with a beautiful man
who never spoke to anyone at parties.
Except one time he held all of us—
my brother and my sister and myself
and told us all he loved us very much.

Christmastime. No one here for long.
Pine needles on the Pine-Sol scented floor.
So little time, still we were there.
Each with a suitcase like another us.
Each minute eaten like another meal.

Two weeks later he had left,
gone back where he was from where it was colder.
Snow gathering on the ornate Gothic bridge
where he once rode his bike, kissed
his first girl, decided to quit his first dead-end job.

Do you think true action is devoid
of thought? A match cracked into an advent flame
somewhere that one night when he was either
generous or desperately talkative,
and then we were emptied from his hands.

Song

Above all things, you must believe.
In hope, and in a denser mysticism,
ossified desire, the underworld
from which no one ever returns.
Or very few.

New Year's Day. I see myself before I left,
folding sheets that later will be washed,
the more-than-perfect guest.
Someone rearranged me when I was asleep.
I awoke to find myself here.

What does it mean to speak
of something we noticed for years and noted
like a list inside our heads and down?
The black oaks in the winter look like brains.
Nervy their insides,

woody dendrites branching into space.
Whether this smoky hue is smog
or some more natural portent (hard to tell),
the curve of it shades me from what I know
is where it always was, and still is now.

The World

No one took care of it: it wintered.
Then you wake up, someone gives you *whatever,*
whatever, pink trees in your head,
silence, silence is the shape of your head.

You wake. The yard. A distinct world.
Not wintering, no. Shoes left out.
Someone approaches, his shyness
like a more forthright self beside his self.

As if redemption could be deliberate.
He seeks redemption, deliberate.
And you seek music, like a motion writ,
like a motion writ in the trees.

You can remember nothing.
A conversation as the house grows dark.
Agreement with your hands.
Agreement. Neglect of the trees.

In Ignorance

Then we were still learning.
Mist covered the college. A blessing
not to see things the same way twice.
Or: listen close and hear the river move.

There remains so much you don't know
about my shoulder.
Questioner, I will teach you,
reaching towards the inadvertent still life

on the table we somehow created
together. Though we swore
not to create anything together.
Wrecked lilacs more colorful than new.

Walking home thinking, I want to teach you
everything, I cannot wait to teach you everything.
As when I was younger, knowing
where was all I wanted to know.

Legend

No one can pay attention for you.
No one can ask the questions you ask
how to ask. So the artist began to make a start
clothing herself in what was given,
entering a home without her mother. Entering
in order not to leave, in order to sit still
for hours. Leaving only in order to return.
Better to scrub floors. The least job as the most
acceptable. Better to do that than to tally numbers
of groceries and philanthropy, than to write
letters of gratitude to the Lord and friends,
than to teach the young to be the old.
No thought of better. Here
the tasks were given. As if to strip a sonnet
to the words that rhyme could make it
the sonnet that it should have been.
Better to paint white walls white again.
Once an artist now she made a start.
She painted so as not to be seen.
The floors were clean. She painted without light.

*

No one can keep you quiet if you don't
say anything. No one can yield a task
if you agree yours is a life of tasks.
So she was called.
The room smelled of nun. That sweat in back
of the clean smell of soap.
As if scents could be in back of other scents.
An early flower from the garden
(not more than one). Two chairs.
This woman tells the artist: make a start.

The vow is that you cannot choose your wall.
The vow requests that you choose your own paints.
The topic is Our Lady at her labor. Sharpen
her spindle, make her mantle blue.

*

Better to scrub floors. The wall was hard.
Too ordinary to be hidden.
The men at the paint store
steered her from blue for no good reason.
Led her to the optic white and black. As if they thought
she wanted to paint herself or make a painting
into which she could go and disappear. This far from worst,
her cogitation only a curtain on the real,
she considered, to turn and return and look at her wall
so deftly painted and seeming complete.
All marks painted out. Her own brushstrokes
perfectly concealed.
To look at that wall and then to get
a pencil out,
and then and only then begin to draw.

*

None can make a start with too much noise.
So she could not. Waiting for the night
she scrubbed floors again.
To begin she copied her own copy of the copy
of Nativity on one of many walls.
She retrieved the Lady's face.
She got the eyes. She got all she could
from what had gone before.

The rest she found
on edges and the corners of the wall.
She could see past paint into the cracks.
She let cracks lead her.
Spindle a spider web
lately descended with its meal inside
she painted over. The stars, shadows from a tree outside
traced and retraced.
The cracks made the mantle.
She saw them from a hundred years ago
or farther. She brought them out.
When the sun broke she was ready for color.

*

Again she began a fresh new thing
on verge of night, thinking
beginning beginning, and then beginning became a thing.
The floor to blend in with the floor
she stood upon. The yarn once eggs in the nest of birds
on that outside tree that threw its leaves for stars.
Spindle left elegant and pointed white
outlined in black ready to be unraveled and dissolved
into a useful cloth. Her clothed in pink. Less mother than young.
Her clothed in a dark petal the dark brick
of this building just a shade less red.
There are no rules for passionate worship.
So the artist rested her last brush and prayed to her wet art.

*

No one can keep a thing from brightness
if that is what it wants.

Art that gets a wall wants to be bright.
This did. The next day in the light
it seemed too much. The colors dark and flagrant,
a garish look-alike of something Spanish
something never planned-upon or liked.
And though her heart
rose and was light as snow that falls slow with
an emotion that might have been pride
denied she saw it covered up.
They kindly said: you do not have to paint today.
She did not start. Art that keeps a wall deepens
into the wall, becomes of it a part.
Sometimes it doesn't mind being covered up.
Exhumed, it has no part
in these matters. Knows it is just paint.

It was spring. Everything coming up.
All things pushing to the surface through the dirt,
flowers and grubs. They were breaking ground
on a new building. Bones were coming up—
nuns that the Order had no record of
Endangered kinds of insects no one knew
the name of and no one cared to save.
So the painting entered the world
competing with so much, not yet a mother.
(No one in this story yet a mother.)

        *

Mater Admirabilis, it is at your beck
she comes, maladroit in her coarse nightgown
with a brush to darken
what is already too dark according to some.

She lights no candle. If she paints
it is by ear and by all slim lights
through cracks from doors outside.
There is moon enough to live by.
At your beck she unfinishes you again.

*

She woke prepared to undo what she did.
(Her mind prepared. Her leg muscles shot.)
Before the morning could start
there was delay. A visitor in the night
who wanted to see how things
were laid out. No need
to edit or avoid. No private places here.
And so he was conducted around,
and so he reached the place where she was,
unbidden, to begin her work
in front of the curious curtain waiting
to be alone in a pose of shame.
Of course he had to ask.
Of course she opened. Of course she had been aware
that even her most recent impulse would darken
in enough time into an ordinary wonder.
A wanted thing.
There would be no more painting over.
There would only be where the wall had been
a Mater Admirabilis, matter most admirable
both wanted and unwanted at her spindle
but lazy with a look of active sleeplessness.
A look of life unable to sit still.

98

Notes

Locus Poenitentiae

The line "and as I raved and grew more fierce and wild" is quoted from George Herbert's magnificent "The Collar." The title translates from Latin as "place of repentance" or "opportunity for repentance." It can also refer to an archaic legal concept which allows parties to an illegal contract to reconsider their positions, decide not to carry out the illegal act, and so save the contract from being voided.

Grave

This poem owes its conception to a short story of the same title by Yasunari Kawabata and is indebted to a conversation I had with Ezra Feldman.

Mammoth Lakes

Mammoth Lakes is a resort town in California's Eastern Sierra. Bob Dylan recorded "Don't Think Twice It's Allright" at least twice.

Song (It is best to be patient and calm)

This poem refers, in its last lines, to Cordelia's first speech in Act IV, Sc. iv of *King Lear*. "Alack, 'tis he: why he was met even now / As mad as the vex'd sea; singing aloud; / Crown'd with rank fumiter and furrow-weeds, / With bur-docks, hemlock, nettles, cuckoo-flowers, / Darnel, and all the idle weeds that grow / In our sustaining corn. A century send forth; / Search every acre in the high grown field, / And bring him to our eye."

Song (You must believe in spring)

"You Must Believe in Spring" is the title of a song and an album recorded by the great jazz pianist Bill Evans (Warner Brothers, 1977).

Legend

The theme and narrative are derived from the story of the creation of the fresco of Mater Admirabilis which hangs in the Trinita dei Monti, a school in Rome founded by the Sisters of the Sacred Heart. In 1844, a young novice, Pauline Perdrau, created a fresco of the Virgin Mary on a wall of that institution. According to legend her original effort was far from beautiful, and was subsequently concealed by her superiors with a curtain. When the Pope visited, he inquired about what the curtain covered. When the fresco was revealed, it had become a true work of art. I have freely adapted the time, place, and personalities of the story.

photo by Deirdre Foley-Mendelsson

Katie Peterson was born in Menlo Park, California in 1974, the middle child of a gregarious Irish-American woman and a dry-witted half-Swede. She attended Stanford University and did graduate work in the department of English and American Literature and Language at Harvard University, completing a dissertation on Emily Dickinson and selflessness. She has published poems and prose in several journals, and has been a visiting Professor of Poetry at Deep Springs College, an experimental school and ranch in the desert of California.

New Issues Poetry

Editor, Herbert Scott

Vito Aiuto, *Self-Portrait as Jerry Quarry*

James Armstrong, *Monument in a Summer Hat*

Claire Bateman, *Clumsy, Leap*

Kevin Boyle, *A Home for Wayward Girls*

Michael Burkard, *Pennsylvania Collection Agency*

Christopher Bursk, *Ovid at Fifteen*

Anthony Butts, *Fifth Season, Little Low Heaven*

Kevin Cantwell, *Something Black in the Green Part of Your Eye*

Gladys Cardiff, *A Bare Unpainted Table*

Kevin Clark, *In the Evening of No Warning*

Cynie Cory, *American Girl*

Peter Covino, *Cut Off the Ears of Winter*

Jim Daniels, *Night with Drive-By Shooting Stars*

Joseph Featherstone, *Brace's Cove*

Lisa Fishman, *The Deep Heart's Core Is a Suitcase*

Robert Grunst, *The Smallest Bird in North America*

Paul Guest, *The Resurrection of the Body and the Ruin of the World*

Robert Haight, *Emergences and Spinner Falls*

Mark Halperin, *Time as Distance*

Myronn Hardy, *Approaching the Center*

Brian Henry, *Graft*

Edward Haworth Hoeppner, *Rain Through High Windows*

Cynthia Hogue, *Flux*

Joan Houlihan, *The Mending Worm*

Christine Hume, *Alaskaphrenia*

Josie Kearns, *New Numbers*

David Keplinger, *The Clearing*

Maurice Kilwein Guevara, *Autobiography of So-and-So: Poems in Prose*

Ruth Ellen Kocher, *When the Moon Knows You're Wandering, One Girl Babylon*

Gerry LaFemina, *Window Facing Winter*

Steve Langan, *Freezing*

Lance Larsen, *Erasable Walls*

David Dodd Lee, *Abrupt Rural, Downsides of Fish Culture*

M.L. Liebler, *The Moon a Box*

Deanne Lundin, *The Ginseng Hunter's Notebook*

Barbara Maloutas, *In a Combination of Practices*

Joy Manesiotis, *They Sing to Her Bones*

Sarah Mangold, *Household Mechanics*

Gail Martin, *The Hourglass Heart*

David Marlatt, *A Hog Slaughtering Woman*

Louise Mathias, *Lark Apprentice*

Gretchen Mattox, *Buddha Box, Goodnight Architecture*

Lydia Melvin, *South of Here*

Paula McLain, *Less of Her; Stumble, Gorgeous*

Sarah Messer, *Bandit Letters*

Malena Mörling, *Ocean Avenue*

Julie Moulds, *The Woman with a Cubed Head*

Marsha de la O, *Black Hope*

C. Mikal Oness, *Water Becomes Bone*

Bradley Paul, *The Obvious*

Katie Peterson, *This One Tree*

Elizabeth Powell, *The Republic of Self*

Margaret Rabb, *Granite Dives*

Rebecca Reynolds, *Daughter of the Hangnail, The Bovine Two-Step*

Martha Rhodes, *Perfect Disappearance*

Beth Roberts, *Brief Moral History in Blue*

John Rybicki, *Traveling at High Speeds* (expanded second edition)

Mary Ann Samyn, *Inside the Yellow Dress, Purr*

Ever Saskya, *The Porch is a Journey Different From the House*

Mark Scott, *Tactile Values*

Hugh Seidman, *Somebody Stand Up and Sing*

Martha Serpas, *Côte Blanche*

Diane Seuss-Brakeman, *It Blows You Hollow*

Elaine Sexton, *Sleuth*

Marc Sheehan, *Greatest Hits*

Heidi Lynn Staples, *Guess Can Gallop*

Phillip Sterling, *Mutual Shores*

Angela Sorby, *Distance Learning*

Matthew Thorburn, *Subject to Change*

Russell Thorburn, *Approximate Desire*

Rodney Torreson, *A Breathable Light*

Robert VanderMolen, *Breath*

Martin Walls, *Small Human Detail in Care of National Trust*

Patricia Jabbeh Wesley, *Before the Palm Could Bloom: Poems of Africa*